Piercing
Thin Air

Tom Wendorff

DEDICATION

This book of poetry is dedicated to my family.

CONTENTS

Introduction

Selected from the many, eighty writings shown here in eight
different clusters. Each cluster a collection of emotions
experienced at the time of writing, yet in some way stitched
together. At times almost piercing thin air, not unlike ebb and
flow of life's joys and sadness.

While readers will discover interpretations uniquely their own.
Relating to individual life experiences, the threads are here to
stitch together your own patchwork.

.

1

Seeking

Seeking, is a life long journey.

A Path To Sensing God's Presence

Love begets faith which requires truth to beget trust
Which becomes the essential element of belief, thereby
Stimulating faith-knowledge to grow into wisdom's light,
Which then provides a sense of God's tangible presence.

In the good soil of love,
Plant the seeds of faith.
Through the roots of belief,
Feed them with truth and
Water them with trust.
Your harvest will be
The fruit of sensing God's tangible presence!

"Lord Jesus, faith in your word is the way to wisdom, and To ponder your Devine plan is to grow in the truth. Open my eyes to your deeds and my ears to the sound of your call; that I may understand your will and live according to It."

The Sound of Footsteps

In the quiet of the night,
In the silence of the day,
In the hall I hear what might
Be footsteps to help me pray.

So softly they keep coming
Their cadence sure and strong.
At first somewhat alarming,
From a long forgotten song.

The door remains ajar,
No person to be seen.
A message from afar
Is there for me to glean.

Maintain respectful silence
States the sign upon the door.
Be still in your compliance,
Bid the footsteps on the floor.
What you seek is not a mystery;
Has always been there for you,
As part of Catholic history
And, Expressed by Vatican II.

Awakening dreams forgotten
The path that leads to Home,
To know you are begotten
And will never be alone.

The I and The Me

I am not my body.

My body is the Me you see.

I am my spirit,

Not as clear to see.

My spirit is eternal,

Forever who I am.

Written in this journal,

While still upon this land.

While my body does the writing

The thoughts are not from Me,

Like the dew they fall from heaven

To the Me that the I can see.

Observing from the outside

The I can see the Me,

To regularly confide

The way the Me should be.

The Me does not always follow

Guidance clearly sent

And so,

That's how, the Me gets bent.

To walk the straight and narrow

To the I, the Me says no;

Except when faced with sorrow

As only a Me can know.

The I composed of spirit

No emotions, no flesh, no bones

For pain to spear it;

Depends on God alone.

Not so the Me, not so;

With one short life to live.

The Me says; let me go,

To get much more then give.

The Me may wish to hide it,

Self-centered as it is.

Convinced that it deserves it.

To the Me that's just how it is.

Not so the I, not so,

Alert to God's command:

"Of your pride let go,

In the dark, take My hand."

Guiding the I to see,

So the Me may hear

Silent words from He;

I and Me, with God near, no need to fear

Heaven Sent

Go where I send you;
Learn to be,
Who you are meant to be.

Use the talents
I gave you;
You have quite a few.

Separate from
The pack,
All they lack.

Inspire
Some others,
Sisters and brothers.

Be My
Secret weapon;
Knife,fork and spoon.

Feast at
The harvest
Be doubly blest.

To your true self
Stay present.
You'll be heaven sent.

If +Then = Peace

If we accept the concept that this earthly planet is the only one, in the known universe, supporting life;

If we accept the concept that a mysterious force causes that to exist;

If we observe the existence of reason, purpose or use in creation;

If we deduce that it is all part of an interwoven plan;

Then we may conclude that the mysterious force is the source of it all.

If we begin to wonder how each person may be part of that plan;

If we observe cause and effect in our surroundings;

If we weave ourselves into the plan;

If we sense the benefits of cooperating with the plan;

Then our soul will find Peace.

Redeemed

Thrice Divine Mastermind, perfectly timeless,

Mysteriously vast, intimate, ever-present.

Providing order, balance and sustenance,

Deserving of all creatures' adoration.

Wayward go I for a lifetime,

Freely abandoning your plan.

Wistful in delusion,

Drawn by the ever-clever

Mortal enemy.

Repeatedly, endlessly,

Welcomed back,

Forgiving my sinful digressions.

Without You I am lost.

With You I am found.

.

Quagmire

Caught in quagmire of uncertainty,
Feet leavened with mud of past;
A mourning dove calls:
"what do I do, what do I do?"

New day dawning
Sun obscured by clouds,
Veil withholding light
And the mourning dove moans.

What do I do, what do I do?
Becomes my plea too.
Dove flies off,
Question aloft.

Do I believe
What I say I believe,
Or do I believe,
What someone said to believe?

Alone, still uncertain;
Recalling breakthroughs past,
"Lord open the curtain
Please answer alas."

Twelve Became Many

Twelve became one,
One became many.
Why twelve to make plenty?

Even if odd to some
Better than any,
For over a century.

Not always welcome,
Overcoming treachery,
Living exemplary.

Charged with rebellion
Their message peremptory,
In truth supplementary.

Inspired from heaven
Ecliptic twelve portions;
Symbolic of Creation.

Chosen by the One
Twelve men inspired many;
Now 110 million times twenty.

Me, Myself and I

Me, myself and I;
Myself also called himself.
The same slice of pie
From now 'til I die.

Three in one;
Sometimes four,
Each day will come
Forever more.

Shave it, save it,
Matters not;
Same peas and carrots
In a pot.

That's who I "r",
Like it or not.
That's who you are;
Believe it or not.

Gaze of the Infinite First Cause

Call as you will,

Gradual or explosively;

Debate continues still.

Big Bang exclusively,

Seven days' bible relief;

State your belief.

Observed thru the haze,

With primordial gaze,

The Infinite First Cause

Created something of awe;

Called Earth

Sprinkled with mirth.

All with simply a gaze!

To the Lord give praise.

Three Is One

Three is One.
Two is a pair.
The Word is One
No need to despair.

ThreeOne is God,
Not one, two or three;
A union is God
Beckoning thee.

Father, Son, Spirit
Thought separately,
Will only derate
ThreeOne; endlessly.

Vast beyond vast,
So how can it be,
God was miscast
For you and for me?

Preaching was simple
For tribe minded folk;
At the time quite ample.
That is no joke.

Two is a pair;
Each disciple joins One
Avoiding the snare,
As taught by the Son!

"the Father and I are one"
Said He.
"Father, Word and Spirit are one"
Wrote John about Three.

The threefold personality
Of the One Divine Being;
Known as the Trinity
By feeling, not by seeing.

2

Promises and Life's Bumps

Promises and Life's bumps, are choices made.

Someday Forever

In a quiet moment together she said,
I wish someone would tell me if
I am going to die, then quickly adds,
I know I am someday,
It is in God's hands.

Will I ever get better?
It has been over a year now.
You are improving daily,
I respond with a lump in my throat.
No, I mean, really better!

We are all working toward that
Praying for help from above without stop.
We hold hands in silence,
Give each other a smile saying,
Only God knows the answer.

So we will do what we can,
Make the best of our time together now.

Someday forever!

Solemn Promises

I take you to be my Spouse,
Dreaming of a life together,
Joined by love that will continue to rouse,
As we grow closer and closer, forever.

I promise to be true to you,
Every day of my life.
Knowing trust is the glue,
That overcomes strife.

In good times and bad,
Whether happy or sad,
We'll stay side by side,
And do it with pride.

In sickness,
We will do, all that we can,
To find a solution
And work on the plan.

In Health,
We shall bask,
As it gives us the wealth,
To go the distance, fulfilling each task.

I will love you and honor you,
Knowing best be done,
For all that you do,
A simple, thank you, at setting of sun

All the day of my life,
Will not be enough,
Honoring solemn promise made,
Even though tough.

Visiting Through Glass

How did we get here, visiting through glass?
Speaking by phone, to help time pass.

Too many sorrows, brought us to this.
Yet hope springs eternal, searching for bliss.

What brought on this nightmare, this time behind glass?
Me thinks it unfair, but da laws rule…alas.

We ask is this justice, separated by glass?
No thoughts of justice, our breath on the glass.

How long…we ponder… must this torment go on?
The price of my flounder!

Perhaps I'll meander; get on God's chosen path,
To live life no longer separated by glass.

When Enough Is Enough

It has been written:
"Forgive seventy times seven"
Allow to be smitten,
Ignore an urge to get even.

When is enough, enough,
Some ask.
Was it time to get tough
Sometime in the past?

We watch a life go astray
Other lives deployed;
And watch in dismay,
No success to be cured.

Missing the obvious,
Blind to the schemes;
Though we were dubious
Hearing false stated dreams

Promises made, promises broken;
The pattern continues,
True agenda unspoken.
Is it time to recluse?

Take your life where you may,
Go deal with your stuff,
It is time to say:
Enough is enough!

Wanting Change

Change is what was said they wanted.
Change from; is what was stated,
Change to; was left unclear.

Change from, articulated
Change to, be calculated
Change for better, left in air.

Change the now, return to what was.
Change the already changed, clear the fuzz.
Change as you like; but not my beer.

Change, change, change,
Change in reparations range.
Change sans grinding gear.

Change, gradual change,
Change, 4 it 2 endure; arrange
Change; be not severe!

The Day Will Come

The day will come,
We know not when,
An accounting for some,
Which I now pen.

Recall the talents
With which you were gifted
And bring to the balance
From the depths you were lifted.

How have you used them,
Or did them abuse?
To yourself remain hidden,
And to others refuse!

Writing your epitaph,
Day after day
Each moment ad libitum;
Thee made of clay.

Yes, the day will come,
Like it or not,
When each is called home
And put on the spot.

How we have lived
The accounting will be
A clear and unvarnished
Personal history.

On the Balance Beam

Tilting to and fro
Pitch, roll and yaw;
Navigating life below
According to the Rule of Law.

In a world
Bereft of hope;
Perverse attachments unfurl
Sliding down the slippery slope.

Actions without balance;
Focused on the "major win",
Consequence-The challenge,
Transgressions leading on to sin.

Back upon the Balance Beam,
Responsibility afoot;
Turning to melodic theme
Wherever dare I set my foot.

Captivity of Freedom

Freedom from ...
Freedom to ...
Free as a ...
Is freedom free?

What comes with freedom?
Does mine diminish yours?
My choice impact yours?
Pro Choice diminish Free Choice?

Who's to say?
Who's to judge?
So many questions.
Is freedom a trap?

Trap it may be,
When not lived responsibly,
Soon you see

3

Memorials, Solace & Encouragement

Memorials, solace and encouragement are needed along the way.

Silent Words

Silent words are spoken,
We do not hear the sound.
Their messages clear unbroken,
A meaning does resound.

Silent words keep coming
Morning, noon and night
Like unexpected humming
To help us through our plight.

Silent words refresh us
Some bring you to your knees,
Sent from one who loves us
And guaranteed to please.

Found amidst the jumble
Of each days earthly demands,
Silent words just tumble
Like the wind across the sands.

Let yourself be open
To the message so softly sent
This silent word just spoken
It's yours and not for rent

is Morning I Cried

　　　　　, I cried
　　　　　.f.
No .　　, hide'
Or sit on a shelf.

The dogs both came
To my side with concern,
Hearing my weeping
They barked to make plain;

We love you they said
In their own special way
So I opened the gate
And am here to say

I cried this morning
And it didn't feel good
It just came, not understood,
Like a man in a hood.

Out of the blue
The tears came gushing
With nothing to do
To bring about hushing.

They stopped on their own
So the dogs went their way
As I picked up the phone
In a most somber way.

Tears will flow as they will,
So let them do so.
It is the dark side of love
And a way to let go.

Hold on to the memories
Let go of the pain.
Cry to be sane!

Four of a Kind

Four of a kind,
Each in her way,
Joined at the hip;
Some people say.

Trained to be nurses,
This group of four.
Fun loving women,
Always ready for more!

Roommates in training,
Sharing all that they did;
Then on to their mission,
Like a star struck kid.

Four of a kind
Each in her way,
Remained best of friends
I can now say.

I knew them all
And am blessed that I did
As we bid farewell
To the one who just slipped.

She left as she wished.
In a soft gentle way,
As she finished her tasks,
At the end of her day.

Four of a kind
Now there are three;
Their love will still be,
I pray with this plea:

Your roommate's in heaven
Preparing some fun
For the best of her friends
So please, don't be glum.

Stay the Way

Shoulders sink lower,
Weight of the years make moving slower.
Weariness shows now,
Life's toll here somehow.

Days come and go, night arrives,
No real change to lighten the eyes.
Stamina gone, how to move on,
Nowhere to go, the spirit now gone.

Too many days, too many nights,
Too many plays, too many sights,
How will it end, nobody knows,
Only our God in the path that He shows.

Show us He will
Realize it of not
Our resolve refills
The half empty pot.

Square the shoulder
Tighten the belt
Before you get older
And wisdom not felt

So many days
So many plays
Yet to be lived
With a spirit that stays

Sweet Newtown Angels

That was the day, a Friday morning
When twenty sweet children
Abruptly went soaring
To a new home in heaven

They left without knowing
How it all happened
And wondering why
They all were now glowing.

Not something they chose
Yet the Light felt so good
After all of the noise
From the man in the hood.

Frightened no longer
At home with the angels
Sweet children of Newtown
That day became angels.

Your Dear One in Heaven

A day comes to a close.
Cannot see the road ahead.
A life comes to a close.
Many a tear shed.

A day, a life, both end;
Both part of the plan.
And the message they send,
To the left behind man.

Is he lost in the dark,
In the shadow of death,
Will life become stark,
Or changes bring breath?

If he trusts in Your will
No reason to fear,
You will be with him still
Of that let's be clear.

A new day will open
And it won't be too long
When the words which were spoken
At the start of a song.

"A new day is dawning."
It will be a gift
From your dear one in heaven
To give you a lift.

Lighten your burden
Shed weights of the past
No time to be sullen
Let your response be fast.

To the needs of another
As she would have done,
Let others just stutter
At the rise of the sun.

Welcome each day
As dark clouds give way,
To do what you can
Let that be your plan.

To help those in need
As you know she would do.
And always take heed
To see others pull through.

White Tablets in the Snow

Row by row they stand,
White tablets in the snow.
Mark the grave of an uncommon man,
Two letters there will let you know.

S.J.; each a man of God.
Each a beloved son,
Enshrined in this hallowed yard
'Long side the stately Campion.

Devoted men, who spread God's word
Where ever they were sent
Worldwide to have Him heard.
Thus to the Lord their lives were lent.

Beneath white tablets
Their bodies rest,
Their spirits forever blessed,
Each an honored Jesuit!

Memorials Large or Small

Looking across the low rock wall
At the markers so low
And the trees so tall.

As we walk down the path
Reading stones so inscribed
Recalling those who have died.

Names carved in stone
With dates of regret
For souls called home.

The markers are varied
In size and design
A sign of their time.

In life some were prosperous
Others were not
Now all share the very same lot

Memorials large or small
Make no difference at all
To bodies beneath.

Their legacy lives on
In the lives they touched.
Do markers really matter so much?

To those still alive
They help us to wonder
About the person who lived worthy of ponder.

Called out of Sight

'Twas this day
Two years past,
That her soul at last
Took leave of this clay.

Beautiful woman,
Both inside and out;
Befriended a cloud
Because of a summon.

Called to come home,
Called by the Light.
Called out of sight;
Called from Troon.

Caring not to leave but
Completing the race,
Content in the embrace.
Can others rebut?

Miss her we do,
Mired in loss.
Making sign of the cross
May Spirit pull us through.

INRI

Jesus of Nazareth:

Became human to bring God's kingdom to humanity.

Became human to reintroduce being human to humanity.

Became a living example of human goodness.

On His last night :

He became the victim of inhumanity,

He became the victim of betrayal,

He became a pillar for torture,

He became the object of ridicule,

He became the substitute for a criminal,

He became named "King of the Jews",

He became the Savior of humanity.

All in one night,

and:

Humanity rejected Him!

Slippery Slope

Slippery slope, tough to climb
Most often quoted
Speaking in decline.

Images abound
To many for recitation
Some may even astound.

Leave to doomsayers
Harkening "the end is near!"
Labeled "instigators".

Slippery slope,
Where are the footholds
Providing hope?

Hope, courage, determination;
These it takes,
To reach your destination.

Look ahead, never back.
Stop and wait,
Tensions go slack.

Footholds appear,
Continue the climb
Into the clear.

Celebrating Lives

Sunday morn
At water's edge;
Now forlorn,
Honoring a pledge.

We hear;
"You are not forgotten,
This or any year".
Promises not rethought-in.

An interfaith service
Celebrating lives;
Casting off paresis.
Blessed in afterlives.

Alone in togetherness,
Registering your name,
Clutching flower stem's tenderness;
Love does remain.

Readings lift skyward,
Clouds give way to sun;
Having gone onward
Your prize already won.

Hearing your name spoken,
Place stem in waiting basket.
This flower a blessed token
So prayerfully does ask it.

"Be free
My dear beloved."
You'll always be
An everlasting love.

Shells

Shells from the seas
Offer praise to God,
If you please.

Each detailed intentionally
At the dawn of creation,
Marking their individuality.

Up from ocean depths,
Protecting task completed;
On sandy shores shells rest.

Scarred with nicks and scratches;
Testimony for some!
To a breeze their praise attaches.

Carried aloft
To nearby trees
Resting on leaves so soft.

Together in joyful chorus
Shells and leaves
Offer praise, from all of us.

4

Growing

Growing, is a never ending process.

This is Who I Am

This is who I am.
I may not be like you,
Doing what I can
To face each day anew.

Living in the present,
For its special gift
Hardly to be wasted;
But not without some shift.

Sometimes to the left
Sometimes to the right.
Always feeling blessed
In the shadow of the night.

That is who I am alright
One who may stand alone
When in the middle of a blight
Always ready to atone.

My sins are all forgiven
The rest is up to me
Providing the attestation
And work for harmony.

St. Joseph is my role model
A man who dealt with change
As he without a squabble
Became the medium of exchange.

In case there is a question
On why these words were written
I close with this impression:
Just do what you've been given.

What do I Write

What do I write
When thoughts do not stream,
When joy has been,
When there is no dream?

What do I write
On this first day of June
With my love out of sight
Like a sky drawn balloon?

What do I write
Looking over the wall
At the markers so right
And the cedars so tall?

What do I write
When there is nothing to say
What do I write
When my soul calls to pray?

This will I write
On this bright day in June
To my spirit's delight
And it will be my tune.

Each day I am blessed
Realize it or not
From becoming all stressed
When I don't feel so hot.

Your Body is not You

You are not your body!
You are your soul.

Your earthly body is leased,
To your soul.
The lease has an expiration date,
Your soul does not.

Your soul is like no other,
Not so your body, not so
Your soul lives forever,
Not so your body, not so.

Your soul has an earthly mission.
One only you can do.
Your soul's Creator loves and protects it.
Not so your body, not so.

Your soul loves and protects your body,
If you let it.
Nourish your soul.
It will care for your body.

Your mind and soul work together,
Your brain and body are joined.
Use your brain to nourish your mind,
Your mind in turn will assist body and soul on your
journey.

In The Eyes of God

In the eyes of God you are who you are,
Certainly not who you think you are.

In the eyes of Satin you are a candidate,
certainly one who he loves to placate.

In the eyes of mankind, you are one of many,
Certainly here to produce more plenty.

In the eyes of a love one, you are more than you are,
Certainly for them a genuine star.

In the eyes of yourself, you are here to be loved;
Certainly, with hands which are not to be gloved.

Be who you are meant to be.
Be the one in the eyes of God.

Shadows + Episodes

Crossing into shadows
Ignoring the sun downs
Entering uncertain
A new drawn curtain.

Awaiting, wondering, shaking
Where is this taking
What path will appear?
Who will be near?

Alone, alone, alone
Leaving to roam
Away, away, away
Without delay.

Writing new episodes,
Now at the crossroads
Begin the epoch
Meaning to ferret.

Pursuit of Wisdom

Wisdom: "the art of balancing known with unknown." (a)
Set compass bearings from what is known
Navigate relentlessly through fog of uncertainty
Use the known to navigate the unknown
Adjust the route as obstacles appear
Relentless pursuit of reality enables clarity
Modify game plan jadishly
Need to know trumps want to know
Dream the goal—play to strengths
Pursue wisdom:
"Living in rhythm with your soul, your life and the divine."
(a)

John O'Donohue – Anam Cara pp. 194+195

Musings on Freewill

Freewill permits me to seek, selectively, within my environment.
Environment influences my curiosity.
Curiosity influences my choices.
Choices lead to learned experience.
Every image and experience, over a lifetime, becomes stored in my memory.
Memory serves future acceptance or avoidance choice; which may bring wisdom.
"Wisdom is the art of balancing the known with the unknown." (anonymous).
Perhaps the very reason for freewill!

Of Core Importance

If apples lacked core,
Then from whence seeds come?
If earth lacked core,
Then from whence magnetic fields come?

If no seeds,
Then from whence apples come?
If no magnetic fields,
Then from whence rotation come?

If no rotation,
Then from earth we fly!
If lost to the motion,
Then tossed into sky.

All for the lack of a core
Apples and all goodbye!
Renew from the core
Whence comes understanding of life.

If life is "gift and responsibility",
Then from whence else its core?
If ignored as possibility
Then magnetic fields may be no more.

Giant Step Forward

Delicate balance;
Self-interest + regard for justice,
Custodial offsetting concupiscence,
Responsibility whilst serving weakness.

Calm facing danger,
Faith overcoming doubt.
Off your seat, on your feet,
Take bold giant steps forward.
Burst through the limitations
Of self-centeredness and edginess.
Stride confidently into your future with:
"Every giant step forward in delicate balance!"

Sitting in a Rose Garden

Sitting in a rose garden on a blissful summer day, mind
wanders through the maze of life's emotions.
As I gaze at flowering plants born from the earth, reaching
toward the sun;
Budding with anticipation,
Some blooming with beauty,
Others fading, petals falling.
Lovingly, skillfully, vine dresser prunes the spent,
awakening new growth.
The Circle of Life witnessed; reality, truth and justice.
In a garden on a blissful summer day!

Pursuit of Nothingness

In the pursuit of nothingness,
The polar opposite of everythingness,
Better than hunting anythingness.

While some call it silliness,
It's the polar opposite of laziness.
Requiring devotedness

To the discipline of not-knowingness;
While bearing witness
With compassionate loving-kindness.

Requires a certain willingness,
Abandoning selfishness,
Adopting selflessness.

Your nothingness
Bringing happiness.

The Silence

In the meantime, in between time,
wandering a path without sound.

Wondering wandering, through
the thicket of noise,
that pricks every cell in the body.

Steadily drawn by unseen light,
step by step, deeper and deeper to
The Silence.

Confused by the veil of concupiscence,
turning, discovering
the path behind gone.

No return possible, move on.
Ever drawn, drawn, drawn to
The Silence.

Your Day Every Day

As you are able live each day completely! Where you are, as you are being precisely where and how you are intended to be; for that day.

Living is your reward or punishment: right now, not tomorrow, next week, month, year or when you die. Not later, right now!

From the moment of your conception until you draw your final breath; awake or asleep, healthy or ill, happy or sad, believe it or not: this is what is.

Live in the moment, you have what you need. When awake * be awake. Do what you are can --- forget or delay what you cannot.   Learn what is good and what is not. That will be your simple foundation to which you return and build upon each day.

Doing what is good will be your reward. Doing what is not good will bring its own punishment.

Enough said!

I Can Not See – I Can Know – You May See

I can not see my eye, only a reflection of it.
I can not see my breath, only feel it.
I can not see my mind, only the results of using it.
I can not see grass growing; only that it did after the fact.
I can not see the thoughts of others, only what they do,
with them.
I can not see the Creator of the Universe, only what was
created.
I can not see what I do not know.

I can know what I do not see!
I can know about the Creator through the reflection of
creation.
I can know the thinking of others by their reflections.
I can know my mind through reflective meditation.

You may see the reflection of my mind by the way I live.

Reflect > Meditate > Live ^

Seeing God in All Things

Keeping the main thing the main thing

A student writes of peer pressure in college
An advisor helps by saying students deal with stress in
different ways
An upperclassman also speaks to the peer pressure to
"party" or be left out
An elder sees a culture of peer pressure as the
underpinning of life's direction
Some social peer pressure that grows, may become the
underpinning of a misguided life
A practice of sing God in all things, brings focus to
keeping "the main thing the main thing"
An understanding of Ignation Spirituality helps withstand
misguided peer pressure
Help in withstanding misguided peer pressure is
Guidance worth giving and living

.

5

Slowing Down

Slowing down, happens, like it or not.

Drawn by the Unknown Mister

At this moment in history,
As I unpack the Mystery
Who we sometimes call God.

Drawn by a whisper
From the unseen Mister.
Who is my Lord!

Should it be a surprise?
As I open my eyes,
Finally seeing what's always been there?

A mountain of care,
Just waiting to share.
A gift from my Lord and my God.

Where have I been?
All of these years,
Distracted by fears?

Perhaps being drawn
Where I no longer belong;
Away for the arms of God.

Growing Down

Growing down,
Gracefully
Without being gone,
Completely.

Content in the moment,
Finally
Out of the torrent,
Gradually.

Need to have more gone,
Happily
Life is what it is,
Naturally.

False self-diminishing,
Prayerfully
True self unfolding,
Wistfully.

Past mistakes forgiven
Hopefully;
Will accept blue ribbon,
Humbly.

Robert K

Robert K, man for all seasons,
Summer, Fall, Winter, Spring.
A complex guy beyond all reason,
Performing in this circus ring.

Robert K, we call him Bobby,
His Summer breeze brings refreshment.
Living well is his hobby;
While he provides the entertainment.

Robert K his step unsteady,
Enters now the Fall of life,
Brought about though hardly ready,
Fighting off a new found strife.

Robert K, now clears new paths,
As Winter brings uncalled obstacles.
Uncertain of the aftermaths,
He'll treat them like: Popsicles.

Bobby K, take your time;
Need only be yourself.
Listen to the wind-chime
Put all else on the shelf.

The Root of Nothingness

Get to the root of nothingness,

That is where you are for God.

It is where you are nothing and God is everything.

Where your ego will not and cannot go.

That is where you form no judgements.

To arrive there, you must die to yourself.

It is from there that you are resurrected.

The root of nothingness is who you are.

The root of <u>nothingness is your true self.</u>

Two Trees

Growing side by side,
Embraced by common breeze;
One robust and tall
The other delicate and small.

Living the Creator's will
In their own distinctive way,
Breathing common air
Washed with common rain.

Nourished by one sun;
Neither jealous of the other.
Sharing joyful sounds,
Suffering common distress.

Much to be learned 'bout neighbors
From two trees.

6

Endings

Endings, as well a part of reality.

Heard In the Hall

Heard in the Hall
Of broken dreams,
To answer the call;
Or so it seems

We'll settle this thing
Once for all!
Were to begin,
To soften the fall?

You said, I said
Followed by my quick retort
I said, you said:
"Let's break it apart"

See; you do't get it
Retort: neither do you
Ho can we break it,
With less holler bellow

Call in the clowns,
To lighten the strain,
There have to be clowns
To ease the pain

And the Crowd Said

He sat in the Temple
And the crowd said:
"Teach us to pray."
He sat in the field
And the crowd said:
"Feed us, we pray."
He healed their ills
And the crowd said:
"Give us more this day."
He criticized their leaders
And the crowd said:
"Make him king today."
He was betrayed
And the crowd said:
"Take him away"
He was offered freedom
And the crowd said:
"Crucify him, today."
He prayed they be forgiven
And the crowd said:
"Crucify him, today."
He rose from the dead
And the crowd said:
"No way!"

The Few Who Remained

They watched me die,
The few who remained.
Now the pain gone,
Evening draws near,
Gently, they take e down,
Caring, loving, weeping.
Remove the nails,
The thorny crown.
Dress my naked boy.
My soul moves on!

Reverently placed in tomb,
Care beyond measure.
Executioners gone;
Eating, drinking,
A day's work done.
My soul moves on!

Body cold as stone.
Darkness enveloped all.
Who will mark this day?
How will they move on?
The few who remained.

Death of a Different Kind

A class of fifth graders was asked to rank a list of fears.

Each child, independently, selected the same number one fear:

"Death of a parent"!

Sadly, there are times when some children do experience the bodily

death of a parent.

More often, children may suffer death of a different kind.

Parental devotion provides care, warmth, concern and safety

It supports growth while enabling shelter.

It is selfless!

It is inspiring!

Without it there is death of a different kind.

Hospice Vigil

Air pump inflates bedding

Music soft, gentle, floating

Notes rising, falling

Breathing

Silence, peaceful, resting

Life's journey coasting

Drifting, floating, dreaming

Angel appear; tiptoeing,

Enfolding, embracing

Escorting

Absolute Contrast

Vibrant, accomplished, admired,
On top of the game,
All clear the road ahead;
Then WHAMM!

In the blink of an eye
EVERYTHING changing!
A TBI
Life is suspending.

Traumatic Brain Injury:
TBI in short hand,
What once was surety,
Now a broken strand.

Snapping closed the lid
On life's well worded plan,
No option for counterbid;
Facing the bogeyman.

Absolute contrast
In the blink of an eye.
Call in the leukoblast,
This is no UTI.
Absolute Contrast

Diagnose the scope
With an MRI,
Praying with hope
It's a small TBI

Images confirm
In graphic detail,
Doctors discern
Treatment scale.

It is what it is
Think what you will
Long lasting paresis:
Brain forgetting a skill.

No Explanation Given

Two fruit trees grow in a garden, the most beautiful
of all trees.
Individually endowed with uniqueness;
One with the fruit of conscience,
The other, the fruit of life.
A sign states: "DO NOT EAT!"
The garden owner posted it.
Visitors wonder why.
No explanation given,
None required.
A self-centered visitor eats from one;
The owner closes the garden to visitors,
Indefinitely!
No explanation given.
None required.

Moving On

From the very start,
Instructions were clear,
Tattooed on the heart,
Year upon year.

Lifelong devotion
To learn sans emotion,
Spanning the decades
Persistence pervades.

Growth the theme;
Home, school and work,
Instilled in the bloodstream,
Building the framework.

When twilight approaches,
What shall be learned;
Are there coaches
For the heart sojourned?

Having learned how to live,
Now, before moving on,
For withdrawal to be advancive;
Learn how to be gone!
Be not caught short
Forgetting how to die.

He Was Alone, Can You Imagine

On a cool April evening, after having supper with twelve friends, the Teacher went out to a garden.

Anticipating some impending trouble, he asked three of his closest friends to stay alert while he went off a short way by himself to pray.

He was alone, feeling the most alone he had ever felt in his life. His father had asked him to take on the atonement required for the failure of many, by allowing himself to be arrested, and be charged falsely for crimes he did not commit.

He was alone, troubled beyond any human understanding. Afraid for his friends and himself.

They, unaware of the impending danger, fell asleep.

He was alone in his agony; keenly aware of the brutality of the times, fresh in his mind the beheading of a dear friend based on the whim of a drunken king. The Teacher fought his fear to the point of sweating blood.

Then, in the distance he heard the sound of voices as a crowd of people was approaching the garden.

He woke his sleeping companions.

To their surprise they saw one of the twelve who had been with them at supper at the head of the crowd.

Assuming it must be alright if he is with them, they just

waited. The one leading the crowd approached the Teacher and embraced him.

It was a signal to the crowd to forcefully grab hold of the Teacher. A scuffle ensued but the Teacher said stop and quietly went with the crowd while the others followed at a distance.

Oil soaked torches in hand to light the way brought an acrid smell to the sweet garden air.

On they went to the high priest who had arranged for the arrest. While on the way, the Teacher asked why the clubs and swords, as he had sat with them in the temple teaching with no sign of conflict. The crowd had no reply, doing only what ordered.

Fully aware of what lie ahead the Teacher then remained silent.

He was alone. No one came to his defense.

Charged with instructing his followers to give to God what is due to God, he was sentenced to death. Death by crucifixion.

Where you there when they crucified him?

Where you there when they nailed him to the tree?

Where you there when they laid him in the tomb?

I can only imagine – I can only imagine what it was to be there and witness such brutality.

I can only imagine!

Imagine I do; over and over;

making no sense of it.

Then I wonder – would I have come to his defense?

Would I have the courage?

Would I say: "Take me; let him go free"?

I can only imagine!

A Blessing

As the curtain begins descending
On the performance of your life,
May Peace, which is everlasting,
Enfold you in the embrace of tender care.

May all your concerns dim,
As the footlights do;
Ceasing to cast shadows
Of the true you.

May the veil of mortality
Begin to be lifted,
Revealing the welcome
Of those to whom you pray;

As you hear your name read
From the book of eternity:
"Welcome good and faithful
Servant"

Pacem!

.

7

Enlightenment

Enlightenment, is a gift, receive it graciously.

Silence, Whispers, Nudges and Bumps

God communicates to us with silence, whispers,
nudges and bumps.
We pray for something we want to have or to have
happen,
We feel strongly about this, hoping for an answer to
our prayer.
Nothing happens; we think God is not answering.
God views things differently and is silent.
We ask again, certain we are praying for something
truly needed.
God views it differently and is silent.
A thought, which seems unrelated, comes to mind
one day.
God works differently, the thought is a whisper.
Unaware of the whisper, we pray our original petition,
again.
Nothing happens.
We wonder why?
We act on the "unrelated" thought.
God is nudging us.
We bump into something unexpected, maybe
unwanted.
Why this now? Then to our surprise,
We have an "ah hah" moment; and see it all.
The silence, the whisper, the nudge and the bump.
Amen!

Safely Reaching Original Purpose

Original purpose softly begun
Building on theme,
Heartbeat strung
Enter the dream.

The call from afar,
To be who we are,
Fulfilling God's plan
As a most devoted fan.

Free from distractions,
Avoiding temptations,
Embracing heaven's attraction
In balanced supplications.

Life's music still playing
Sounding tempting calls.
Original purpose saying,
Give God your all.

Musings on Techniques Observed in Current Use

Using:
Free will to alter creation.
Emotion to outsmart intelligence.
Power to crush weakness.
Free will to become enslaved.
Gifts of creation to ignore them.
Strength to become weak.
Evil to outsmart good.
Addiction to overcome common sense.
Distraction to outwit concentration.
Delusion to overcome clarity.
Medicine to become ill.
Activity to dismantle peace.
Ignorance to avoid responsibility.
Denial to be affirmed.
Faith to instill doubt.
Hope to instill despair.
Love to instill dependence.
Direction to create confusion.
Texting to avoid speaking.
E-mails to avoid eye-contact.
Warnings to suspend involvement.

Make Time To Meditate

Make time to meditate. Start with three minutes.
You can do it!
Find a quiet spot and sit, eyes OPEN,
Pick an object in view, concentrate on it.
As thoughts come to mind (they will) let them go.
RETURN TO THE OBJECT.
Three minutes – no more – no less
Every day (same time if possible) for a full week.

Increase Time To Meditate
Find a quiet spot, sit erect eyes CLOSED. Notice
your breathing.
Not WHO you are but THAT you are.
Listen to the sounds that surround you

Select a single word to come back to (like: heart, love
or give)
As thoughts come into your mind, let them go.
RETURN TO THE WORD.
Five minutes _ no more – no less
Every day (same time if possible) for a full week.

Evaluate Time To Meditate
Take time to evaluate.
Sit quietly with paper and pen.
Write whatever comes to mind.
Three minutes – no more – no less
Read what you wrote,
Two minutes – no more – no less
Decide if you want to continue,
One minute – no more – no less.

Meditate On That

That you are human,
No more, no less
That you have a life mission,
No more, no less
That you were gifted talents,
No more, no less
That the Creator loves you as you are,
No more, no less
That you are responsible,
No more, no less
That you be free,
No more, no less.

Light of the Spirit

On a sunny summer morning,
We sat, facing each other.
Two on a journey.
Not a journey to a far off place.

No boarding passes in view,
Itinerary drawn from a lifetime.
Clouds of the past
Giving way, to new light.

Chairs provide comfort,
Silently holding secrets,
Voiced by travelers
Past.

Now, unfurling
This day;
As the sail
On a mast.

Journey continues
Through bleakness of winter,
Warmed by
Light of the Spirit.

Deo gratias

Flash Frozen Convictions

Flash frozen opinions,
Engraved in mind as convictions.
This age of mass media;
Broadcasts sans criteria.

Asserted with confident assuredness,
Not a modicum of unsureness'
To balance the scale;
Should boldness fail.

Sure what was said is right,
As it came to mind just last night.
Without question a true manifestation;
Since widely broadcast by CNN.

No need for dialogue or discussion
With mind simply a pincushion.
Ingesting the blogs
Only adds to the fog.

Ancients without instant access
To developing messes,
Required discussions,
To formulate opinions.

Not so the modern, not so.
Armed with media radio
Twenty four - seven news.
And so it goes. Flash frozen conviction!

Life Is Its Own Celebration

Life is its own celebration!
Celebrate birth, celebrate death,
Every life, every day.
It is a gift: the present.
Live in the present – the now.
Misuse or disuse it not.
Every experience, each emotion
Is there for a reason,
Not a commotion but for locomotion.
Learn from the past
To celebrate the now.
Every now becomes a past
Leading to a future.
There is joy in sorrow,
Tears blur the vision.
Like rain bringing new growth,
Washing clean the pain.
Just remain,
In the now!

Found Amidst Jumble

Found amidst jumble
Everyday demands,
Anything but humble
Aha the soft commands.

Is it any wonder;
Missing all the signals
Day by day we flounder,
In the world we mingle.

Lost in the climb
Of achievement,
In the search so blind,
Reaching for agreement.

Where, when, how...
The true-self appear?
Peak into the jumble
Ever so near.

Peel off the wrapper
The false-self you wear.
Beneath find the chapter,
"Get out of the glare".

As you unwind,
All you did;
There you'll find
The self-that's been hid.

8

Light Hearted

Light hearted, have fun.

Hemi and Harley

Hemi and Harley
I got `em both!
Call it a parlay
I am happy to boast.
As I roar down the highway
With nowhere to go
What looks like a fly-a-way
To those in the know.
Hemi and me
We make quite a pair
Add Harley and see
The wind in my hair.
Then what a surprise,
As I wiz past a tree

And focus my eyes
On a cop behind me.
With his light flashing red
Brought a lump to my throat
And quick thoughts to my head
On my truck there's a note:
"Got Hemi" you see
And so does he
In his Dodge Charger three.
There will be, no ticket for me!

Murder in Westport

Last night there was a murder in Westport.
A premeditated, stealthily executed act.
The victim was ill prepared to escape the danger.
There Is no evidence effective aide was supplied by
onlookers.
Strange as it may appear to some, just a normal
occurrence to the naturalist.
While it has saddened some who learned of it.
Adding to the puzzlement of it all is the fact that the
most likely murderer, is protected by law.
Not so the victim!
What little protection is afforded to a baby born to
graveyard parents, while the ravenous killers prowl
about is search of their next victim.
It is in their DNA you say.
The circle of life or something like that.
Perhaps, but still sad to see the remains of a baby
deer, killed by the coyote pack.

Falling in Love

Feeling
almost
lightheaded,
laughing
inside,
never
guessing
it
near
Love
outshines
virtually all
emotions.

Who

Who am I to say?
Who am I to know?
Who am I to judge?
Who am I to?
Who am I?
Who am?
Who?
-?

Steps to Finding Peace

FINDING PEACE

Frustration
Invitation,
Navigation
Inspiration
Negation or
Gravitation?
Perspiration;
Evaluation or Aspiration.
Contemplation
Explanation

Intention

Intention begets action,
Action begets perception,
Perception begets reception,
Reception begets trust,
Trust begets faith.
Faith requires trust,
Trust requires perception,
Perception requires observation,
Observation begets belief,
Belief builds on intention!
May all your intentions be trustworthy

Angels in White

There was a time
When nurses wore white;
Head to toe,
Day and night.
There was a time,
T'was not long ago,
I'm told it is so,
That nurses wore white.
Training was tight;
In class and the ward,
Building the skills
Of the angels in white.
With the passage of time
The white was replaced
By solids and prints.
For most, that's ok, while
Training remains tight;
And so it must be,
As patients deserve
The best care in sight.
I must confess,
I miss the white
Yet solid or print,
For me, you remain

Angels in white.

Rockwall Pine

Carried on the breeze
From the not too distant mother,
A white pine seed
Settled in a spot like no other.

Crevice in rock wall
Provided safe landing
Moisture, heat and soil;
Perfect seed sprouting.

Briar bush sent leaves
To hide the sprouting seed
From ever hungry birds
And other creatures.

Seasonal weather brought
A blanket of snow
Protecting seedling
From harsh blasts of wind.

Safe in the womb of rock
Seedling grew to sapling,
Drawn skyward
On a warm spring day.

Alas, a small yet sturdy
White pine tree,
Named:
Rockwall Pine.

When Sinks Were White

When sinks were white
And cars were steel,
Right was might
Church bells peal.

Stores closed on Sunday.
Church doors burst wide open,
For the families who together pray;
As God's words were devoutly spoken.

Phones had wires,
Were attached to walls.
No one had blow-dryers
And there weren't enclosed malls.

Folks bathed once a week
On Saturday evenings.
Talc the powder technique,
Scented and pleasing.

Bath tubs were white
Back in '54
Life was alright
Atop the linoleum floor.

Gone are the days
When life was that simple,
Pre social media craze
Plus, every new wrinkle.

Sinks now are steel,
Cars fiberglass white;
Expressways congeal
Both day and night.

That's all I have to say
About that!

A Million Times

A million times a million,
How high the numbers go,
On and on;
Additions to the glow.

Somewhere there hides
An answer.
Above the skies
Said sister!

Un-calculate-able,
Chimes brother.
Beyond the stellar table;
Why even bother?

Want to know or
Need to know,
Is at the core
We'll show!

More good than bad
We humans, worldwide.
A million times more glad,
Then the other side.

Shine on sisters & brothers
Your glow offsets gloom.
With evil don't bother;
Let joy fill every room.

ABOUT THE AUTHOR

Tom Wendorff was born in Brooklyn, N.Y. into a Roman Catholic family. The church has been an important part of Tom's life as far back as grade school. In high school the Marist Brothers provided a positive impact on developing his spiritual life. It set the foundation upon which exposure to Jesuits in college taught him to question, debate and dig deeper into scripture for answers, while living in a secular environment.

Through the years his ability to "see" and "feel" God in an ever growing number of places and things has taken place. Much of his poetry is a reflection of this. Interestingly, years as a senior business executive instilled a keen sense for intuitive listening. Combining that with studying the writings of Thomas Merton, Thomas Keating, William Barry S.J., Jon Kabat-Zin, Anthony DeMello S.J. and others continue to influence his work.

Tom lives in a cottage in Connecticut where he continues to study and write, while actively participating in Ignation Spiritual Direction

39566928R00072

Made in the USA
Middletown, DE
19 January 2017